How to Make & Keep Friends: More Tips from our 2015
Blog Posts

Copyright © 2016 by Donna Shea & Nadine Briggs

Contents

Welcome to How to Make and Keep Friends!

Many kids struggle with social nuances which can make it difficult for them to form lasting friendships. To help kids during those times, parents and kids often need quick social skills advice that is easily understood and even easier to do in the moment. Our tips have proven successful for children with mild to moderate social challenges. While some of the children who have learned these techniques have a specific special needs diagnosis, many do not. Any child who struggles socially and needs a little extra support will benefit from our tips and strategies found in our books.

In March of 2015, we started a blog on our website at www.howtomakeandkeepfriends.com to offer fresh tips and strategies for kids as well as parents. We are happy to share all of the posts from this past year with you in this e-book towards our mission of social success and friendship for everywhere!

Being an Upstander

March 2, 2015 by Nadine Briggs

Whenever we read about incidents of bullying in the media, we usually hear reference to peers being "upstanders' or "bystanders." The difference being that a bystander stands by and does nothing to stop the bullying contrasted by the upstander who steps in and stops the negative interaction. Being an upstander is encouraged but many times both children and adults do not really know the language to use to be an upstander. We have had parents, teachers and chaperones share stories where they knew that they should intervene but either did not because they were not sure what to say, or tried to stop what was happening only to find that they had inadvertently fueled the flames.

We suggest for both kids and adults to keep a calm demeanor when intervening as an upstander. As emotions grow this is not always easy to do but is the most effective means by which others will listen. Getting upset or yelling will create a larger problem in an already difficult situation. Kids could just say "Not cool," or "I'm not going to be a part of this and why are you?" The upstander sentiment may need to be repeated and may be met with insults but the upstander should continue to calmly, but assuredly hold his or her ground and keep repeating the same upstander statement. If the situation allows, they could follow up by having the victim leave with them to join a friendlier group.

Parents, teachers and chaperones can use the same serious yet calm authoritative voice and say "I see what you are doing, it is mean and I want it to stop," or "That is not okay and it needs to stop now." Notice the I-based language in the first statement and the use of *that* instead of *you* in the second statement. Adults should not say "Hey, that is bullying and you need to stop." Labeling someone as a bully could make the situation worse. If the group tries to deflect your intervention by claiming that they are *just kidding* or the like, the adult should stay firm. "That is not funny and it needs to stop now."

Left Out at Recess?

March 8, 2015 by Donna Shea

When coaching a child who expresses that he or she feels left out at recess, we suggest one simple change in the child's approach to other children that may increase his or  her chance of being included. If a child is being left out during recess, this change of language will often do the trick.

We teach children to change the yes-or-no approach of asking "Can I play with you?" to the more effective statement of "I'd like to play with you." We have seen how powerful this change in phrasing is in how other children respond to the child making the request to play. We also coach children to take this one step further and also say, "Tell me what you are doing," or "Tell me the rules of the game." Children who find themselves excluded may have a history with peers of being welcomed into play, only to the have the child joining in begin to try to take control of the group or change and complicate the rules. It is important for the child that is requesting to play to conform to what the other children are already doing. These changes can result in a more inclusive recess experience.

Handling a Flip Flop Friend

March 15, 2015 By Nadine Briggs

"Mom, I don't know what's going on with Marybeth. She came over this weekend and we had a blast but she wouldn't talk

to me in school today. She was acting like we're not even friends. She does this to me sometimes. What's going on?" Marybeth is being a flip flop friend. This is someone who is nice to your child sometimes and not nice at other times or who hangs out with your child only when no one else is looking or available.

Rejection of any sort is painful but rejection from a friend is both rejection and betrayal. We hear from kids who experience flip-flopping behaviors from peers as early as elementary school. Any time someone has a mean moment toward your child or diminishes your child, it's important that your child stick up for his or herself. Here are some comeback lines to suggest that your child try:

- "Hey, Marybeth, I got a weird vibe from you this morning, what's up?"

- "Marybeth, I need to talk to you about something. I feel like you're friends with me only when you feel like it. What's up with that?"

- "Hey Marybeth, did I accidentally upset you or something? I noticed that you ignored me this morning and I wanted to be sure we were cool."

Marybeth may make an excuse; say she didn't see you or act like she doesn't know what your child is talking about but that part doesn't even matter. She'll know what your child is referring to and now she knows that he or she is going to address it when she flip flops. If it turns out Marybeth doesn't care and continues the flip flop behavior, it may be time for you to support your child in re-evaluating how much time he or she wants to spend with Marybeth or if he or she wants to continue the friendship at all. Our Real Friends Checklist may help your child determine who is or isn't being a good friend.

A Real Friend:

- Wants to get together with you when you are not in school.
- Is trustworthy and acts like a friend all the time.
- Makes you feel good about who you are.
- Doesn't try to change you or make you feel bad.

- Listens to you.
- Likes you for you.

Opinion or a Put-Down?

March 23, 2015 By Donna Shea

"I can't believe you still watch that baby show." "You really listen to her music? She stinks!" "What is that weird stuff your mom put in your lunchbox?"

These kind of put-down statements happen between kids all the time, diminishing what another child enjoys either by accident or on purpose. Either way, these types of statements are hurtful. By teaching kids a simple change of phrase we can help them learn to respectfully disagree. In order to spare someone else's feelings about something a child doesn't personally enjoy or agree with, we teach the use of *in my opinion* before he or she says what he or she thinks. Kids can also be coached to say "it's not my favorite" as another way to soften their opinion.

- "In my opinion, that show is too silly for me. Do you watch _____?"

- "In my opinion, her lyrics don't make sense, but do you listen to _____?"
- "In my opinion, PB&J beats sushi in my lunch."

Throw Out a Friendship Feeler

March 30, 2015 By Nadine Briggs

Jim: "Wanna come to my house? How about tomorrow?"

Frank: "Um, I can't tomorrow. I'm busy."

Jim: "How about the next day? Or the day after that? I'm around this weekend too. Can you come this weekend?"

How can you tell if someone is being truthful and is just busy or if the friendship has not reached that point where he or she is comfortable hanging out or having a playdate? This is a hard call to make for all kids and especially true for kids who may have trouble reading social cues. If a child misreads these signals, he or she may also find him or herself experiencing outright rejection to the invitation. We teach kids to do something we call "throw out a friendship feeler" and then pay close attention to the response. Here are some ideas:

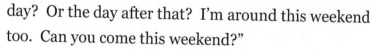

"Want to hang out and play some video games sometime?"

"My Dad just put up a new basketball net. Maybe we can shoot some hoops one of these days."

"My sister just gave me all her Barbie™ stuff. I thought you might want to dig through the box with me?"

We all hope for the wonderful responses of, "Sure! When?" or "Yes! Let me ask my mom when I can come." However, if a child is met with a response such as "Gee...um...I'm not sure," or a similar vague reply, we suggest a child wait a while longer before trying another "feeler." If the second feeler is not met with a clearly positive response, a child should leave the door open by saying, "Okay, let me know sometime when you can come over" and then think of another peer to feel out for a play date.

Invisible Squares & Imaginary Bubbles

March 30, 2015 By Donna Shea

Joey reaches in front of another child to grab a building block piece to the tune of, "Hey, give that back! I was using it!" Zoey wants a magic marker to draw her picture and when she reaches for it, bumps another child's hand, receives an angry look and a "You just ruined my picture!" retort. Brayson is forever getting in trouble at recess for playing too roughly and not being to maintain safe space.

Kids who struggle with personal space do better with a visual demonstration, or a more concrete way to think about maintaining personal space. We talk to kids about the imaginary bubble (or invisible square fence or force shield) that surrounds each person. Some people's bubbles are smaller and they do not mind if you get close, but other people have larger bubbles. If someone has taken a step back, that person's bubble has been popped and it is important to take a step back or stop coming closer. It can be helpful for a child to practice with a bubble that can be seen, such as a hula hoop. It is also helpful for your child to hold his or her arms out and turn in a slow circle near you or in a small group of kids that are practicing how close is comfortable with each other – if he or she bumps someone then he or she is too close. A safe distance while standing is about an arm's length and if a child is sitting, a forearm's length.

When doing table work or playing with building blocks or drawing materials, you can help your child with personal space by describing how each person has an invisible square in front of them at the table. It should be assumed that any materials in that square are being used by that person and if your child desires to use something in front of something else, he or she should ask if that item is available and wait for an answer without reaching in and grabbing. Kids who struggle with personal space issues are truly unaware that they are too close to others so it is important to give them tools and tricks to understand where their body is in relation to others.

The Verbal Mosquito

April 13, 2015 By Nadine Briggs

"Can I have snack? What time is Dad getting home? Can we go get ice cream? When can we go to the movies? What time is it?"

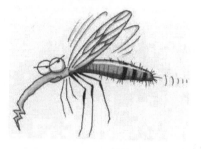

Some kids ask a lot of questions. We have heard parents say things such as, "We call her Question Girl because she asks so many questions."

Asking questions is welcome and important when a child really needs answers, but some kids will ask rapid-fire questions of others and seem to revel in the joy of asking rather than really requiring an answer. This type of questioning can grow tiresome quickly. Adults tend to have more patience with a child's questions than his or her peers. The brutal honesty that most kids use may gain a child a less-than-polite response to the constant interrogation.

When a child starts to pester other children or adults by following them around and asking repeated questions, it can feel a bit like a "verbal mosquito."

The constant questions can eventually sound like a buzzing in the ears of his or her family and friends.

Kids who have this questioning tendency are going to have trouble socially. Coaching should always be kind and come from a point of understanding and redirection. We suggest:

"Wow, you sound super curious today! That was a lot of questions. My ears are starting to feel a little tired, so it is time to hold on to any more questions for now."

If the questioning is taking on an angry tone and the inquisition is getting heated, we suggest saying, "This question is not an emergency. It is time to wait patiently for an answer."

If the questioning is repeating in a loop, we suggest saying "I'm hearing some of the same questions that I already answered. Let's take a minute to try to remember my answer."

Kids who tend engage in verbal mosquito-ism are usually driven by anxiety. When the anxiety is addressed in a productive way by changing the conversation topic and adults being caring and kind, the questioning should stop. Kids may also need guidance in terms of which questions to ask out loud versus which one they can wonder about quietly without asking, versus which ones they can answer for themselves using their observation skills.

A Compliment Is a Gift

April 19, 2015 Donna Shea

I gave my young friend Justice a compliment the other day when we were working on a jigsaw puzzle together.

She replied with a comment to the effect of, "I'm not really <u>that</u> good at it." I gave her two more compliments on how great of a jigsaw puzzle solver she was (which she is – so much quicker to see where the pieces go than I am). She gave both of those compliments back to me as well.

How many times do we all give compliments back? "That's such a pretty sweater." "Oh, this old thing? I just grabbed it out of the closet." "Those brownies are delicious." "Not really, I cooked them a little too long."

I looked at Justice and I said, "I feel sad and a little hurt." She wanted to know why and I said, "Because you are giving my present back to me. A compliment is a gift, and when you give it back to me, it says that you don't like my gift." She thought for a minute. I then said, "Next time I give or someone else gives you a compliment, just try saying 'thank you'." She did. And then she did again. And then we were both smiling because it felt better. The gift was given and happily received.

The Chronic Apologizer

April 27, 2015 By Nadine Briggs

"I'm sorry! I'm sorry! I'm sorry!"

Our hearts go out to the children who have the triple-sorry mantra as their "go-to" phrase when they think they have committed a

social faux pas. These kids feel like they have made an egregious error and feel terribly about what they have done. We want kids to acknowledge their mistakes and apologize for purposeful wrong doings. However, the kids who tend to triple-sorry usually use it as either a reaction to something that can usually be answered by just saying "okay," or as a habitual phrase for avoiding working through a problem. For example, a small correction from a peer or an adult such as, "Those aren't the rules of the game," or "Running isn't allowed indoors," can be answered with "okay" and do not require an apology.

Imagine how a child must feel if he or she goes through life feeling the need to constantly say he or she is sorry for something. It is important to teach kids when a true apology is warranted (when something is done in a purposeful way) and when it is not necessary (an honest mistake). For example, a child who deliberately destroys another child's block tower on the floor by kicking it needs to understand that an apology is expected for not working through the preceding problem in a way that worked better. A child who accidentally knocks over that same tower can say, "Oops, I didn't see that there. I can help you fix it." In this way, we can help children to be less hard on themselves.

Children also use the triple-sorry as a habitual way of avoiding working through a problem. In this scenario, we coach kids on showing us actions that can address the situation rather than providing an avoidance phrase in the hopes that the problem will disappear. Children can learn that everyone makes mistakes and the ways to acknowledge, make amends and apologize as needed.

Know Your Audience

May 1, 2015 By Donna Shea

Our young friend James has a keen interest in and amazing knowledge about appliances – particularly washers and dryers. Many kids have a specialty with a particular topic – it's what we call his or her "awesome." The world is such an interesting place with all of the different "awesomes" that people have. James may very well own a large chain of appliance stores someday. Maybe your child's "awesome" is trains, or history, or cooking.

Where a child runs into social difficulty is when he or she forgets, or doesn't realize, that not everyone shares the same awesome. He or she may not be able to read the signals that the person he or she is talking to has lost interest. Sometimes that person may nod and say "uh-huh" or "yup" and the child misses the tone of voice or facial expression that indicates they are done with the topic and takes these statements as a sign of continued interest.

James was talking to one of the teen helpers at one of our centers last week. He was explaining all kinds of things to Miss Kate about front loaders versus top loaders. He was telling her about the different features as well as the cycles. Miss Kate was producing those polite signals of "uh-huh" and "yup" and James was missing the cues. I politely stopped him for a moment and said, "James, I have a question for you. Based on what you might know about teenage girls, how interested do you think Miss Kate is in this topic?" James thought about for a moment and responded, "About 10%."

I said, "I think that's a really good guesstimate of interest. Do you think you've given Miss Kate less than 10%, just about 10%, or more than 10%?" James replied, "Oh, waaaayyyy more than 10%." I said, "I think so too. So based on what you know about teenage girls, what could you do next?" James said, "I could change the subject or ask her a question about what she likes to do." And he did.

It is important for us to celebrate specialties and "awesomes." It is also important for us to help a child to become a little bit more of a generalist in every day conversations and for the child to think about and know his or her audience. A great way for a child to learn to tease this out is to ask questions to gauge interest before beginning a conversation about his or her favorite topic. For example, a child who is into Star Wars™ could ask, "Do you like Star Wars? Do you like it a lot or just a little?" By checking in first, they will know to adjust how much they should talk about that topic. James, who's specialty is much more unique for a child, may have an easier time saving this particular topic for when he's visiting with family, doing a report for school or taking field trips to chat with appliance salespeople at appliance stores and trade shows.

Walk Strong. Talk Strong.

May 11, 2015 By Nadine Briggs

How a person feels about his or her self is evident by the way he or she walks and talks publicly. Our bodies and voices are broadcasting our inner feelings without us being aware of the messages we are sending. When we visit schools and present workshops to classrooms for our bullying prevention program, we explain to kids the importance of walking and talking strong. We role-play with kids exactly what walking and talking strong looks and feels like. Confident kids are less likely to be bullied.

Talking strong is delivered in a moderate volume voice with shoulders back, a stand-up-straight posture with head up and a confident look on the face. A strong voice may be a bit lower in pitch than a joking voice would be but it is definitely not shouting. Take a few moments to practice talking strong with your child by mimicking a weak voice, followed by a too-strong, nearly shouting voice and then settle in to the voice in the middle that is confident and strong.

Walking strong is important for kids to understand and practice. When teaching kids this skill, we have the kids walk around the room with us in three different ways. First, we have the kids walk the way someone who gives the appearance of a victim or under-confident person would walk. A victim body posture would be small steps, shoulders caved inward, and hunched over with a worried, meek or sad look on the face.

Next, we have kids do the exact opposite and walk with maximum swagger as if they are way too cool for school. We generally get lots of strutting around at this point in the exercise and, of course, a lot of giggling.

Then, we settle everyone into a walk that is in-between victim and swagger. Here we teach the kids to hold their shoulders back, and heads up high, but not too high. Steps are taken with purpose but no stomping. Hands are relaxed and may be put in pockets or thumbs hooked on pocket edges or lightly crossed in front for. The walk may include the tiniest bit of swagger.

By practicing the look and sound of walking and talking strong (and we encourage kids to fake-it-until-you-make-it), your child will become less likely to be the target of a bully and will build his or her inner confidence.

Click <u>this link</u> for an interesting Ted Talk about the research that explains why this is effective.

My Big (Gasp!) Sword

May 18, 2015 By Donna Shea

Miss Donna here. So, I am
learning to play Dungeons &
Dragons (or D&D as I am
told by my experts). That in
and of itself is a story, but
for another time. Although,
I will share that my

character's name is Faun Tree Elf and I think that I
am slowly beginning to get the hang of things, despite
the confusion I have over all of those different sided
dice.

My D&D experts who are teaching me are a
social group of four awesome tween boys. As the
adventure progresses, we are, of course, battling a
band of Kobolds (to which, I suggested that we run
away, but no one agreed with me). In the heat of
battle, one of the guys (newer to our merry band of
adventurers) shouted out, "I'll get him with my big
a$$ sword!" I'm not sure whose face looked the
funniest or whose gasp was the loudest. Probably my
teen assistant Michael's. The two kids who have
known me awhile came in a close second. We all
became involved in an awkward moment. At first, I

didn't say anything and almost decided to just let the moment pass, but then decided that there was a nice opportunity for social coaching.

I froze the game play for a minute. I told the player wielding the sword that I wanted to explain something and that no one was in trouble. I went on to admit that I'm a little bit old-fashioned and asked if anyone knew what "mixed company" was. I received the correct responses of boys and girls together as well as adults and kids together. I went on to talk about the fact that I initially had thought to let the moment completely pass, since if I was taken out of the equation and it was just all boys playing, that the comment was absolutely just fine. This is how a group of guys would and should play the game. However, since we decided that I qualified both as a girl and as an adult, that we should adjust the language to reflect being in mixed company.

One of the most difficult skills to teach children, especially those who tend to be very rule-based, is those times when a word or an action is socially on target, and the times when it's not. These types of social rules, the kind that we bend, are moving targets, and with practice and patience, kids can learn to hit the mark (and Miss Donna to conquer a Kobold).

Longing to Belong

May 25, 2015 By Nadine Briggs

Me: "Do the other kids like him?"

Teacher: She hesitated and then said "no" with a heavy, sad sigh.

This was part of a conversation I had with a wonderful first grade teacher after a classroom visit for one of the kids who had been attending my social skills program for two years. I knew him really well and he had made great progress during the time that he attended the social group. In the past, he used to have seemingly random mean moments toward other kids but we had moved on from that. Though his social skills were not perfect, he was able to get along quite well with others in social group. He still had his quirky moments, but he was a really nice boy and a great friend to the other group members.

The school visit was prompted by a conversation with his mom shortly after the school year had started. He had just begun going to a new school.

>Me: "What's lunch like for him?"

>Mom: "Oh, he says that he's so hungry, he really just wants to sit and eat."

>Me: "How about recess? What games is he playing and who is he playing with?"

>Mom: "He says he just likes to run around at recess."

>Me: "Does he mention any specific friends?"

>Mom: "Well, no one in particular but he says that he has friends."

>Me: "I'd like to see what's going on at school. Those responses may be red flags and I'd like to be sure he's adjusting well in his new school."

The visit was enlightening to say the least. When we observe, that's literally all we do. We take notes the entire time but we do not interact with any of the kids, even the kid who knows who we are and is wondering why we're in his or her class. We usually just say that we are there to help out the classroom teacher.

So I watched. I watched this wonderful teacher with her math stations creating a fun, social, math lesson for the class. My little friend sought out a math station to participate in and found two of the boys playing a dice game. "Can I play too?" he said. "No," said the kids. He seemed to shake it off and went off to find his own math activity with some flash cards. I couldn't hear all he said but he interacted with two girls who gave him a few seconds of their time before walking away from him. Another boy was approached to see if he would use the flash cards with him. He spoke to him a little and the boy walked off to interact with other kids. My friend returned to his seat, alone with the math flash cards while the activities were winding down. The whole while, he was unable to find someone to do a math activity with, and in turn, missed out on the learning that occurred. It was heartbreaking.

The kids went out to recess at that point, but I had seen enough and needed to speak to the teacher.

Me: "I have a question for you. Do the other kids like him?"

Teacher: She hesitated and then said "no" with a heavy, sad sigh.

Me: "It looks like the kids essentially shun him. They don't appear to interact with him or they give him a few seconds of their time before walking away. It this usually what happens? "

Teacher: "Yes. He had some personal space issues at the beginning of the year and it turned off some the kids even though he doesn't do that stuff anymore."

Me: "It's not okay for them all to ignore him. As a class they're shunning him and it needs to stop. The class needs a lesson in social skills."

The teacher hadn't realized that this type of exclusionary behavior was actually whole-class bullying by shunning. Thank goodness this teacher was incredible. She did talk to the class and everything changed. One class lesson in including others resulted in him being a valued member of the class. He started to play tag at recess. When they played ball, he actually got the ball passed to him by his classmates. By the end of the school year, he had five true friends who would come to his house for play dates. Just one thoughtful lesson on how to treat others in a first grade classroom and one boy's entire life changed.

My young friend didn't need me anymore. He didn't need a social group; he just needed a second chance.

Absolute Thinkers: Parts Versus Whole

June 3, 2015 By Donna Shea

"I <u>never</u> get a turn." "My mom <u>always</u> gets me here late." "No one <u>ever</u> wants to play the game I want to play." "I lose <u>every</u> time."

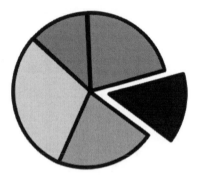

Does your child revert to absolutes when something is frustrating or doesn't go his or her way? Does he or she not see that while the current situation might be frustrating or not to his or her liking, that he or she is caught up in a bad moment rather than an entire day?

My 11-year old friend, Noah, was demonstrating some of this type of absolute thinking at a social group recently. Things were going along well and the boys had been engaging in having fun playing the Wii. We had been playing a favorite board game of Noah's for the past couple of weeks and after we had finished with the video game he wanted to play that particular game. Unfortunately, the other boys in the group had temporarily tired of that game and wanted to play something else. Noah became upset and stomped out of the room, saying, "No one *ever* wants to play what I want to play."

In social coaching Noah, I first empathized that I understood his frustration in that no one was interested in playing that game on this particular day and how disappointing that was for him. I expressed my concern that he would leave the group, get in the car and tell his mom or dad how awful it had been. I labeled what was happening as "whole time thinking" instead of "thinking in parts."

I reviewed with him what I had observed during the course of the group and the specific moments I saw him enjoying himself with the Wii and the other boys. I pointed out nice conversations he had engaged in and times when I saw him laughing and joking. We talked about having a "bad moment" rather than a completely bad time. With a little patience and explanation, Noah was able to work his way through the absolute perspective to a more flexible and realistic description of the day's experience.

Fire Pits and Flashlight Tag

June 8, 2015 By Nadine Briggs

I love hanging out around fire pits. It's like camping but without having to sleep on the ground. The crackling fire, Jiffy Pop, marshmallows, s'mores (quite possibly the best treat, ever!), it's all so...summery! I especially love it if the yard is full of kids playing flashlight tag with some adults to keep *me* company. When I was a child, all the kids in our neighborhood used to play hide and seek every night in the summer with a huge tree in front of my house as home base.

The best times always seem to be those that aren't planned so it's a good idea to keep a bagful of barbeque skewers and marshmallows on hand so you're ready to socialize on a whim. Marshmallows can be stored in the freezer so you can stock up. Outdoor socializing also means that you don't have to clean your house. Not much preparation is required and it creates such wonderful memories.

Group games are so much more exciting when played in the dark. This type of excitement can be a bit too much for some kids, though. Here are some tips to prepare kids who may have sensory issues or are fearful of the dark:

- Describe the game while it's still light outside and let them know that they don't have to play if they don't want to.
- Try pairing kids up into teams or pair up a tentative child with an older child.
- Set guidelines for safe boundaries and use visual reminders (ex. Park your car at the end of the driveway, put a lawn chair at each corner of the yard).
- Tell kids that they can take a break when needed and relax with the adults by the fire pit.
- Provide some bubbles and balls for kids who don't want to play flashlight tag and set them out in a well-lit driveway or area of the yard.
- You may have to emphasize that sometimes your child will win and sometimes another kid will win.

How to Play:

- Play this game in a dark house at night or in a safe place outdoors at night.
- Find a place to be base.

- Choose one player to be "IT".

- The person who is "IT" waits at the base and counts while everyone else hides. Hiders can move around during the game.

- "IT" searches for the hidden players with the flashlight. The flashlight must stay on at all time and cannot be covered.

- Meanwhile, players try to run to the base without getting caught.

- Players are tagged if "IT" spots them with the flashlight and calls out a player's name.

- Each tagged player is sent to the base to wait until the very last player is caught.

- The last person tagged is "IT" for the next game.

- Set a time limit for the game, if no one is tagged during that time frame, switch the person who is "IT".

Safety Tips:

- Have an adult mark-off the game area.
- Play in the safe area. Canvass the play area in the daylight. Mark off dangerous holes and low hanging branches, and remove all potential hazards such as yard tools, toys, clotheslines, etc.

- Provide everyone with a flashlight for safety purposes, but only the person who is "IT" keeps theirs turned on.
- Players should not leave the game area without telling an adult.
- Do not throw anything at other players.
- Watch for cars. Never play near a busy street or intersection.
- Apply insect repellent, especially in wooded areas.
- Have an adult monitoring the fire pit at all times and have a hose nearby

Call some friends, break out the marshmallows, check the junk drawer for flashlights and enjoy!

Do the walk...do the walk of "out."

June 15, 2015 By Donna Shea

Some of you who are our age might have an old Dire Straight's song playing in your head now. Enjoy the tune and keep it in mind if your child struggles with getting out when playing games.

One of the biggest challenges that some kids face at recess and on playgrounds is the ability to be "out" in elimination games. For some kids, being out causes angry meltdowns, tears or arguing with other players that delay the game and remove the fun.

We've come up with a strategy for kids that we call the "walk of out." In our social groups, before we play a game that involves getting out, we walk through and practice how that looks. It makes it even more fun when our teens or we ourselves play along too. The "walk of out" is meant to make getting "out" fun by emphasizing the drama. Kids have fun acting as dramatic as possible as they remove themselves from a game. Here is a short video of kids who volunteered to help in demonstrating how we do it (and a great big thank you for their assistance and their parents for permission to share.)

By encouraging this over dramatization, the thing that can cause anger and meltdowns, being eliminated, becomes fun instead!

Are YOU Having Enough Fun?

June 21, 2015 By Nadine Briggs

Yes, you. I see you turning around to see if I'm talking to the person behind you. I mean you! Are YOU having enough FUN? Have you asked yourself this question? Do you go out

with your significant other or friends? Do you laugh regularly?

Many of us are too consumed by kids and worrying about them to focus on fun. We work too much and are often overwhelmed by life. We strive to help our kids achieve active and fulfilling social lives but what about us? Are we too busy for friends of our own? It's okay to take a moment and assess the level of fun in your life.

If it's somewhat lacking, then it's time to make a change. It's time to make a concerted effort to add more laughter and lightness. Not sure where to begin? Here are some ideas:

BBQ – burgers and hot dogs with a salad. Gatherings with friends don't have to be a ton of work or anything fancy. It's the being together that's important.

Call a friend for dinner and a movie.

Grab coffee with a new friend – if friend is new to you and you're feeling uncertain, having coffee is a relatively short encounter and you can decide when you are ready to leave without being awkward.

Have a buddy over to watch a baseball game or the Bachelorette or whatever it is that you like.

Schedule a game night – play LCR (Left, Center, Right dice game), Dominoes, Rummicube or have guests bring their favorite game.

Your social life is just as important as your kids' social life. If you lived in such a way that you had an active social life and were generally happier because of it, isn't that an amazing example to set for your kids? Wouldn't you be more well-balance and even more prepared to deal with those times when you're overwhelmed?

Say "yes" to laughter. Call a friend. Grab lunch. Have a game night. Go on a date. Make some days just about you.

"That" Kid

June 27, 2015 By Donna Shea

I am the mom of *that* kid.

But I wasn't always. My growing up years were as typical as they come – the white picket fence kind. Sure, I got into it with my little sister now and again, but that was pretty much the extent of any family conflict. I was an A student, and spent my school life in band, chorus and drama club. I was a girl scout and sang in the choir at church. I babysat, worked at McDonald's with my friends and I followed the rules.

I got married a year after graduating high school with visions of white picket fences and a natural continuation of my experience of family life. Little did I know the path would be so very different and a couple of years later, I found myself in a world I didn't recognize, expect, nor had the tools to navigate. I became the mom of *that* kid. The one who:

Did not sleep through the night for 14 long months. The one who was climbing out of his crib by 9 months and could get over two baby gates stacked on top of each other. The one who I found on top of the refrigerator, coloring on the ceiling. The one who our neighbor found in her kitchen at 7 AM in the morning at 2 years old. The one who at 3 years old found a screwdriver and unscrewed all of the legs on the TV stand. The one that we had to lock in his room at night and caused us to install dead bolts inside all of our doors to give us enough time to reach him before he escaped. The one who I had to put on a wrist leash and endure the stares of strangers before those cute little backpack ones were created. The one who set fire to a mattress while we were on vacation with my family. The one that I spent all of those toddler and preschool years just trying to keep alive. The one we had to medicate at only four-years old for his own safety.

That kid hated to cuddle, needed to sleep on top of a running dryer in his baby seat and was happiest in his bouncer. He couldn't stand being put down in the grass to play and flung sand, rocks and anything else he could find to fling. He screamed himself purple during his first haircut and when he wanted his blue shorts at the beach. His non-stop, inquisitive nature caused librarians to glare at me, playgroups to be impossible to attend and I became very adept at the walk of shame.

I asked for help. His pediatrician said, "he's just fine." Translation: it must be you. I brought him to a child psychologist at 3 years old. He immediately destroyed a jigsaw puzzle in her waiting room. She got angry with me. I thought, that's why I'm here. Translation: it must be you. We lasted at family functions for about 45 minutes before I heard, "he just needs a good spanking." Translation: it must be you. I became a failure to that kid.

That kid started school and the calls from teachers started too. "Mrs. Shea, your son (fill in the blank) today." Every September, I would put him on the bus and pray that this year was going to be different. It never was. Attending school functions often entailed more walks of shame. The police came to a basketball game after he called 911 on the pay phone as a prank. The police never once came to my house when I was growing up. We became *that* family to the town police, the school and other families in town. That kid finally gave up in 7th grade after his teacher (in a TEAM meeting) told him that he was simply lazy. That kid started down a path of self-medication and substance use. Our family fell apart.

Hopefully, we have a better handle on *those* kids then we did 25 years ago and I have made it my life's work to sit with moms of these kids who struggle with what was unnamed for me – sensory processing challenges, anxiety, ADHD and all that goes with that – and say to those moms, "It's not you. It's not him. It's this."

That kid has turned into the most amazing young man who I not only love as his mother, but respect as a person. He lives on his own, earned his GED, works hard and attends college. We all stopped the shaming of ourselves and each other and turned it around. *That* kid is the father of my beautiful granddaughter. He and her mother have created a wonderful version of a white-picket fence childhood for her. And when she has children some day, and if things turn out not the way she expects, I believe she'll have our hard-earned tools for the job.

*Note: I have two sons who struggled in different ways – for ease of writing, I compiled experiences with both of them into one. For those that might be interested, I did a thesis project in college on the experience of mothering an ADHD child. It's a research paper (translation: a little dry) but here it is in its entirety: <u>Mothering-Peter-Pan</u>

In like a kitten, out like a lion...

July 5, 2015 By Nadine Briggs

My assistant motions to me that someone is crying outside. She is an eight-year-old girl who I know well and has been participating in a group at my center for several months. She loves coming and has made many new friends. We were closed for two weeks...just enough time for her to regress.

By the time I reach her, she is in the throes of a panic attack and clinging to her mother. Her brain is in full fight or flight mode and she is not able to overcome these feelings or listen to suggestions for how she may calm down. Giving strategies to her at this point may, in fact, make the situation worse.

After a bit, the crying starts to slow down and the opportunity to intervene presents itself. I think hard about what I can do to gain her interest. I suggest that she come look at my secret craft box and see if there is something she wants to make. Mom quietly leaves to go to the waiting room, unnoticed. Now is the moment when I know I have her. She starts telling me all the things she is going to make from materials in the craft box. Her face is still wet with tears and her eyes are red.

While she is exploring the crafts, I show her how to make a worry kit that she can use when she feels upset. She says "I really need one of these." The kit is a plastic baggy containing:

Gum – chewing can help relieve stress
Soft Pom-Pom – to use as a fidget & to feel the softness
Rubber pencil grip – to use as a fidget & to squeeze
Play-Doh – to squeeze & create
Personal power card (click to download <u>kitten and lion personal power cards 2015</u>) to remind her that sometimes she might feel like a kitten but really there is a lion inside her. She is strong even when she might not feel like it.
Dragon Breath craft <u>(click here for how to make)</u> we made this dragon craft so she can learn how to breathe deep.

I remind her of the <u>incredible five point scale</u> and that she wants to start the deep breathing before she reaches a five. I tell her that next time, she should start to deep breathing when she feels the tears **start** to come.

We add notes to her "I CAN" can to celebrate that she was able to separate from her mom. The cans hold notes of accomplishment that kids can look back on and realize that they are able to overcome obstacles.

She leaves with her anxiety kit, all of her crafts, and a new sense of strength in knowing that she can overcome her anxiety. In a moment of contented reflection, she says "If I cried the whole time then I wouldn't have had any fun."

She came in like a kitten, found her personal power, and went out like a lion.

Transitions are tricky and sometimes, sticky!

July 12, 2015 by Donna Shea

Difficulty with making transitions is a common theme that I see with many kids at my Center. There have been numerous upset

moments over the years such as over needing to finish a Lego project or a drawing when everyone else has already left. Some parents mention a major struggle getting their children to come to their social group, only to have a great time when they arrive. Children who push or shove in the recess line, run away from recess aides or who have a hard time bringing their energy down to return to class are all demonstrating tricky transitions. How do you help a child learn to turn tricky transitions and into terrific transitions?

Initially, it is important to build in a little extra time when possible to practice making transitions. I try very hard to not have to be somewhere immediately after a social group when I have new members that are learning this skill. When there isn't extra time, here are a couple of visual or auditory cues that I have found help children make successful transitions:

This is a simple clock that I use window markers on to show kids time moving. We have "green time" or free time until 5:30. At 5:35, time becomes yellow and we start getting our brains to think  about the fact that a transition is approaching and make sure we finish whatever we are working on. When we reach "red time," we clean up and get ready for parent pick-up and we are "done" at 5:45 PM. The kids now tell me when we are getting to yellow and red, and after a week or two, transitions go more smoothly. When possible, I also let kids save a Lego project for one week to work on the next time, or allow a few crayons to be "borrowed" to finish a picture at home.

These are a couple of handy little apps that I use as timers for transitions, turn-taking and anytime we need to containerize time or become unstuck. I have a Droid, but I'm sure that  there are many similar apps out there for the Iphone.

The app on the left is a visual timer that counts down one or two minutes. The red will disappear as the timer moves, allowing kids to see how much time is left. The one on the right is an egg-timer app and allows up to an hour on the timer. When times runs out, it clucks like a chicken and the kids have found that funny, making transitions much less painful and eliminates the need for me as the adult to use my voice or repeat myself in order for the transition to happen.

Here is a link to a similar visual timer app on Google Play: Flip's Timer

Here is a link to the egg timer app on Google Play: Get Cracking

Most importantly, it is most helpful to teach a child the word "transition" and it's meaning from an early age. It gives a name and meaning to the thing that he or she may be struggling with. Here is a little social story for kids on tricky transitions that you are most welcome to use with your child who may sometimes get caught up in tricky or sticky transitions.

<u>Transitions Are Tricky...And Sometimes, Sticky!</u>

Being True to Your True Self

July 19, 2015 By Nadine Briggs

Donna and I decided that as we write this blog, we would tell our readers more about who we are. Donna shared her story in the powerful "That Kid" post. As I sat down to write my story, I realized that mine has many parts and disclosing all those parts will take more than one blog post. Donna would say the same and we look forward to writing about and sharing the real experiences that brought us to where we are and our passion for helping kids.

When I was in college I had a strong interest in psychology and considered becoming a psychologist. As I thought about the type of job I would likely get as a psychologist, I knew that I would hear about really sad things as part of that job. I have always been very sensitive in nature and didn't feel like I would be able to separate myself from the sadness of others if I was to work as a psychologist. I majored in business instead with a minor in psychology.

In my senior year of college, I had an internship at the local TV station where I got some exposure to how the station measured performance and success. From there, my first job was at a research company that did marketing research for TV shows and news stations. I moved from my home in upstate New York to Boston to pursue this new career. I found it exciting to be part of new TV shows for PBS and I worked with kids in schools and in their homes to see how much they liked new shows. I moderated focus groups and did lots of math.

I worked for another research company that required me to do even more math but the companies that I analyzed were Ocean Spray Cranberries, Kraft General Foods, and even Ben & Jerry's. I was with Veryfine Products as head of their research department and was on the team that created Fruit2o. I was successful in this world filled with math. I wore suits, carried a briefcase and click-clacked my high heels through many airports. I used to fly to Chicago, attend meetings and fly back all in one day. I was driven and ambitious and reaped the rewards that this type of life provides. I thought life was pretty good and that my future was bright. But you know what? I hate math. I have always hated math and doing math as my job was not my true self.

On December 10, 1996, my life changed in ways that I could never have anticipated. I went into labor with my first child, and I will spare you the difficult details of that day, but when my baby was born, she didn't breathe. She was taken to a side table and a team of doctors and nurses swarmed into the delivery room. She wasn't crying and I thought my baby was dead. I kept asking "why isn't she crying?" No one answered me. "What's wrong with my baby?" Still no one answered. My husband and I started to panic until finally, one of the doctors said "they aren't ignoring you by not answering. They are trying to figure out what's wrong." Her heart is what was wrong. Megan was born with Down syndrome and a very severe heart defect.

Her presence in my life caused a seismic shift in my neatly-packed lifestyle. Within 24 hours of her arrival, I was planning and prioritizing her life. I said to my husband, "Social skills have to be first. She has to be socially appropriate or no one is going to take the time to get to know her. Communication is second and the rest is what it is."

Megan's birth brought me back to being my true self. Teaching social skills to kids is what I was meant to do with my life. If only I had known as a college student that you handle the sad stories by focusing on the helping, I would have been helping others much sooner.

I am grateful to Megan for teaching me be true to my true self.

Make Manners Matter

July 26, 2015 by Donna Shea

It is my belief that respect is something that cannot be demanded and I purposely avoid using the word respect or phrases such as "you are being disrespectful" or "you need to respect me" when I work with children. I

Kindness Counts & Manners Matter

cannot make a child respect me. I cannot force anyone to respect me. Respect is something that I have to earn by my own words and actions. Respect is something that is only created if the feeling is mutual between parties. Respect can be won and respect can be lost. A great deal of the success that Nadine and I have with children is based on cultivating mutual respect.

Manners however, is something that I can insist on. Manners is one of the main ingredient of respect. We can use manners whether or not we respect or agree with someone. Manners are basic, and I am distressed by how often in our culture these days, good manners are missing in our interactions.

In spite of all of the difficult times I had raising my boys, they were never rude in public or to other adults. In my summer program this year, I am witnessing or personally experiencing multiple occasions of lack of manners – from young children barking orders at me rather than using please and thank you, elementary-age kids leaving a trail of debris, spills and trash behind rather than cleaning up after themselves, abuse of community items, digging both hands into a bowl of community snacks and taking unreasonable amounts, as well as tones of voice that if I had ever used with an adult when I was a child would have had consequences that I am glad I never faced from my own parents. A last straw for me this week on the manner subject came when children in my waiting room hissed at me (in front of both parents) when I offered a friendly greeting. So, I am hopping up on my soapbox for a moment on this subject.

We have had several discussions on manners with the kids in the program in the last couple of weeks. All of the kids knew and could tell me what good manners are. We reviewed the expectations for manners each morning and in social groups. We talked about the difference between making social mistakes and working hard to use good manners and the purposeful choice to not use good manners. I told the kids I never have a problem with mistakes or giving reminders when needed. I do have a problem with deliberate acts of defiance and rude behavior after reminders have been given.

I am careful to make sure that kids first know my specific expectations and that they know what good manners are and that I am happy to help them learn what I mean by good manners if they don't. I also reinforce to the kids that unlike school, this is my space and those that deliberately choose not to try and use his or her manners will not be invited back. The premise of our social coaching is based on kids being receptive and willing to work at it. One of the boys asked me if I had ever "disqualified" anyone from coming back to my Center and I affirmed that was indeed the case, but that he did not have to worry as long as I could see that he was trying.

When I have a group of kids that are working on remembering and using basic manners, I implement a positive reinforcement plan for using good manners with each other. Many times, kids need a small reward to motivate them towards the changes we would like to see. In turning the tables to focus on when good manners are being used and a small treat at the end of the session for using them, I see an immediate increase in pleases, thank you's, cleaning up and friendly tones of voice. It doesn't take long for kids to understand that in creating an environment that is full of good manners, not only is it much more pleasant for all, kids discover they actually receive whatever it is they were seeking much more easily – an item by asking politely, positive attention from peers and adults and a feeling of social and behavioral success. I am always surprised by how simple it can be to change the focus to positive and how hard kids will work for the price of a small piece of candy (or other small treat based on food restrictions).

Many times, I have noticed that kids with special needs have learned and display terrific manners. For these kids, the challenging part is when peers or the rest of the world does not return those good manners in kind or with the expected response. However, I think that it is also important that we be careful not to give our special needs kids a "pass" on using good manners and to keep the bar and our expectations high. We are doing kids a significant disservice when we do not insist on learning and using the basics. The world will not like our kids if we don't. Kids have it hard these days and the times they are growing up in are very different from ours. Not holding kids accountable for using manners only makes it harder for them in the long run. Manners make us more likable. Manners are crucial for life success. Make manners matter.

Is There a Bully in Your Brain?

August 3, 2015 By Nadine Briggs

Our minds never stop thinking. We are constantly bombarded with an ongoing dialogue from within our own minds. What are we saying to ourselves? Is all of it true? Are we always nice or kind to ourselves?

We all agree that bullying is bad and never to bully anyone, but how often do you or your kids think:

"I'm not good enough."

"I'm going to lose," or "I'm a loser."

"Why should I even try? I'm not going to be able to do it."

"She isn't going to want to play with me."

"He'll think I'm weird if I talk to him."

"I'm so stupid," or "I'm in idiot."

Whoa! When we really think about it, we speak this sort of language to ourselves on a regular basis. If anyone else ever said similar things to us, we would consider that person as a bully. It's a good thing that we have control over our thoughts, because our own internal bully has got to go!

Teach kids to listen for this type of self-deprecating thought pattern and change the channel in their brain.

Instead of: "I'm not good enough" say instead "why not me?"

Change "I'm going to lose.", to "I will try my best."

Instead of, "Why should I even try? I'm not going to be able to do it.", change the brain to say "I'll just try my best and if I can't do it or I'm not the best at it, I know there are other things I'm really good at."

Rather than thinking that you are stupid, consider what you might be missing and tell yourself that you will figure out the issue with further thought or assistance. Remember that if you take a chance and the person doesn't want to play with you or thinks you are weird for talking to them, he or she is not somebody who you want as a friend anyway.

We have control over our thoughts. It's not going to be easy to change this pattern of thinking, but we can learn to overcome the the bully in our brain. We wouldn't treat our friends that way, let's not treat ourselves that way.

Storming the Castle

August 9, 2015 By Donna Shea

Some kids have a difficult time with being shy and joining in. Some kids have mastered the social finesse of working his or her way into a group of children already playing together. Some kids

demonstrate the storming-the-castle method of joining in.

Castle-stormers want to join in, but lack the ability or awareness to do so in a way that is not perceived by their peers as a hostile take-over. Castle-stormers come in quickly, too quickly, and hijack the game or toys that the other kids are playing with in their efforts to be part of the group. This social term popped into my brain one day when I watched a trio of boys literally storming a castle toy that a couple of girls were playing with in our social group. A conflict over the toys quickly erupted, and I used this term to describe to the boys the social scenario that had just occurred as we worked out a truce (a picture of our peaceful group treaty is below).

Social coaching your castle-stormer includes giving him or her the right words to say that will find him or her easily included by peers. This is as simple as teaching your child to approach the child or children he or she wants to play with and say, "I'd like to play too. What are you doing (or what can I play with)?" It is important to point out to your child that when he or she joins in play-in-progress, that he or she is the one who should conform to what is going on and not attempt to change or complicate the activity.

With this small change in approach, your castle-stormer can build that bridge across the moat to a great play experience.

New School Anticipation: 20 Thoughts to Manage Back-to-School Anxiety

August 17, 2015 By Nadine Briggs

Worry comes about when we don't know what to expect, and that is certainly true for any new school year. In particular, kids  who are changing schools can really struggle with anxiety. Kids worry about the new and unfamiliar environment and this can cause sleepless nights, tears, difficult behavior and other signs of high anxiety.

When my daughter, Megan, was making the move from the elementary school to the middle school, she was extremely nervous. Her anxiety-driven tears came early in the summer and we needed a strategy to help her cope. A big part of giving her the tools to cope was to provide a way to process the change in her mind.

One summer day, we stopped by the middle school to take a few pictures and look around. We took  pictures of the gym, basketball court, lunch room, and even a few staff members allowed us to snap pictures of them. We placed the pictures in a small photo book so she could look at them often over the summer months. We also added thoughts about the transition to remind her that not all new things are bad and that she was going to be just fine. The book had the following notes:

- It's OK to be nervous.

- Just be yourself.

- I will see old friends and make new ones.

- I love school!

- Just breathe.

- I will get used to the new school.

- It's OK.

- Focus on fun things.

- Stay calm.

- Try not to think of things that make me feel stressed.

- The middle school has dances and I love to dance.

- Be myself.

- The other kids are probably nervous too.

- Focus on the work.

- I can do my best.

- I can be strong.

- It's not that big a deal.

- If I get lost or confused, there are people there to help.

- The teachers will help you.

- I'm ready for this.

Use photo books, social stories, reminder cards, cell phone videos and stories of how you yourself managed a big move. Whichever tools you use are up to you. The important message is that new is not bad, just different and that new becomes the familiar in no time at all.

Trapped in a Den of Ogre Pokers

August 24, 2015 By Donna Shea

I just came home from vacation after facilitating a 6-week full-day summer program at my Center. Each week brought me new kids to meet and new challenges to coach. Was it fun? Mostly. Was it easy? No. Did I lose my patience? Absolutely, I'm human.

There were many days over the summer when I felt trapped in a den of ogre pokers. What is an ogre poker? It is a term that we use when we are talking about kids who engage in annoying attention seeking behaviors or refuse to leave someone that he or she is in conflict with, alone. For some kids, it is the rush of getting attention from peers or adults. To the ogre poker, negative attention fills that need more quickly and easily than positive attention. For other kids, they get stuck on a small conflict and rather than taking a break, continue to try to engage the peer until a bigger problem grows that didn't need to exist. Ogre pokers are problem enhancers. We seek to teach kids to look at a problem and think about his or her role. Is he or she currently a problem solver, a problem creator, a problem enhancer or a problem victim (getting caught up in someone else's problem).

Ogre pokers can find themselves not well-liked by peers or adults. An ogre poker can cause an otherwise calm and caring person to feel exasperation, frustration and anger and well...to lose his or her patience. I found the best way to stop an ogre poker in his or her tracks, is to remove the attention he or she is seeking. I would have the child take a break away from the group and relocate to a boring area, stayed within sight and did not engage visually or verbally until the child opted to discuss with me what was going on, and what needed to be done in order to re-join the activity.

If you come face-to-face with an ogre poker, you can attempt to defuse the poking by saying "I think you want my or _____'s attention. The way that you are going about getting our attention is not working. What would be a better way to get our attention or what you need?" And if you get caught in a den of ogre pokers? Try to keep your sense of humor, have a boring location at the ready, find someone to temporarily cover for you, and have chocolate available.

Understanding Leads to Understanding

August 31, 2015 By Nadine Briggs

"I'm concerned that the teacher will peg my kid as the bad one."

"I'm worried that the kids won't like my child."

When we send our children to school each fall, we want them to feel comfortable, accepted and liked. We want them to feel like they are interesting, intelligent and competent. Some of our kids, though, will behave in ways that can be difficult for others to find likable. They may talk too much, be impulsive, have trouble with personal space and sound boastful or arrogant. The awesomeness that they possess may not be readily apparent.

Teachers have the tough job of trying to meet the needs of all their students and patience may be limited at times. Classmates and educators may react negatively to how our kids interact with others, especially if they don't understand the underlying reasons as to why kids act the way they do. When someone has a physical issue or limitation that can be observed, we understand why they are unable to run, write or speak clearly. If a child uses a wheelchair, for example, it is a clear sign that they have issues with using their legs. Kids with social challenges, however, do not have such a symbol. The challenges they struggle with can be thought of as their invisible wheelchair. So what to do?

Explain. Sometimes explaining how and why your child behaves the way they do to teachers can be enough. The teachers can gently, and at the appropriate times, educate peers on social issues. For example, my daughter Megan, who has Down syndrome, used to use self-talk as a processing strategy. She would be working on a craft with a friend while talking out loud to herself as she worked through the steps. The other child didn't know if she was talking to them or not. An adult can easily anticipate the confusion in this scenario and explain that she is talking to herself. Once the classmate knew why she was talking, she would become more understanding and even ask her if she was talking to herself or to them.

In my social group, I have a boy who was in kindergarten last year. His teacher would say some upsetting things to him. His mom gave me several examples of comments she had made about how he shouldn't be making any mistakes. She also told the class that she expected bad behavior from this boy but not out of the other kids. At 5 years old, her sharp comments began to erode this little boy's self-esteem.

He had some annoying behaviors in class and by the end of the school year, this teacher was clearly frustrated to the point of not being able to keep in the negative thoughts she was having about him. There is a secret to him, though, as there is to all kids. They have to know that you like them or at least a part of who they are. If they feel disliked, that can create more difficult behavior. This little guy is very anxious and he really needs to know what is going to happen and when. If he asks when snack is and is told "in a minute", he is going to count to 60 in his head so he knows when a minute has passed. Understanding a few things about this boy would have likely resulted in the teacher helping him with this anxious thoughts and would have decreased his behavior.

For many years, I have completed a personality profile for my daughter. Teachers love to get the insight as to who she is as a person. Armed with details about her life, they were also able to tailor academics to things that interested her. Give her a math word problem about a planning a party and you will have her full attention! The personality profile template that I have used is located <u>here.</u> Some parents have given the same information with a concise one pager. Others meet with the teacher at the beginning of the new school year, bringing a classroom gift of hand sanitizer or some other needed supply, to chat about the best way to interact with his or her child.

Friendly parents who appreciate the difficult job of teachers, who provide information on their child and open the door for ongoing and productive discussions throughout the year, can set the tone of collaboration. Those parents know that understanding leads to understanding.

Act Your Age

September 6, 2015 By Donna Shea

Have you ever found yourself using or thinking the words *why don't you act your age* with a child? The answer to that question, more often than not, is that the child cannot on a consistent basis, meet developmental expectations.

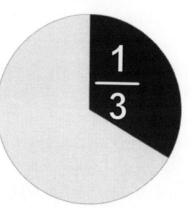

It becomes even trickier when a child is intellectually and cognitively very bright and academically successful. Our expectations are that his or her social-emotional development should match or exceed his or her chronological age. When I see a bright child struggling with behavioral challenges and lowered self-esteem, I see the gap where adult expectations are higher than what that child can deliver. I also listen to parents talk about how there are often smooth periods of time when their child does meet expectations, followed by days or weeks where he or she does not. So we also become confused when the child is able to perform or behave developmentally on target sometimes, and other times we are using the demand of *act your age*.

I see a great deal of this type of chronological versus developmental gap in many kids. Because I have raised two sons with ADHD, I understand it the most with kids who carry that diagnosis, but I also see the same gap in kids in my daily work that are struggling with anxiety, or have a social communication challenge. Is your child attracted to playing with younger or older children most of the time? This is a sign of that gap, as your child may be developmentally in the place of younger children who are more his or her peers than his or her classmates, or look towards older kids to guide the play.

I encourage parents who find themselves thinking thoughts about *acting your age* to change their expectations of their child to a child that is 1/3 chronologically younger. In using the 1/3 rule, we can begin to understand:

- The 4-year-old that still tantrums as a toddler might.
- The 5-year-old that engages in parallel play or has difficulty sharing.
- The 8 or 9-year-old that occasionally resorts to whining or a babyish sounding voice.

- The tween who still enjoys shows or toys that much younger children enjoy.
- The teen that avoids typical teen activities or learning to drive a car.
- The high school senior that isn't at all ready to leave home for college.
- The late-twenties adult who doesn't understand why all his friends want to get married and buy houses and why he doesn't have any interest.

How does the 1/3 rule play in to helping kids make and keep friends?

A social group can help your child learn the skills necessary to close the gap. In a group of peers, a facilitator can work with helping children learn the skills to move from parallel play to collaborative play, point out how certain actions are not what kids his or her age typically do to solve problems, and offer a greater age range of peers to play with. If your child gets along great with slightly younger or older children, those friendships should be encouraged. I often explain to kids (and parents) that if all my friends were required to be exactly my age, Nadine would be my only friend.

For some kids with ADHD, a medical intervention, when carefully considered and appropriate, has helped kids perform better not only academically, but socially with their peers. I can remember a child that Nadine and I had in our summer program who was struggling mightily in getting along with others, managing his personal space and a host of other socially damaging actions that were symptomatic of his ADHD. His mom mentioned to us that he used medication during the school year and we suggested that he try it the next day for camp. The change is his social interactions and his likeability by peers was visible and remarkable. I am by no means pushing the use of medication and it is an important decision for each family, but only noting that we have observed the a significant decrease in the social developmental gap in some children using this form of treatment.

I think the most important thing we can do for kids who are developmentally lagging a little in their social-emotional development, is to recognize when the 1/3 rule is in effect and adjust our expectations accordingly. In any situations where a child is struggling or you find the words *act your age* crossing your mind, take a minute to assess if your child is responding in the way of a younger child and intervene the way you would for that younger child, while consistently working on the skills your child needs to bridge that gap.

Friending the Enemy: When a Bestie Becomes the Bully

September 13, 2015 By Nadine Briggs

Research abounds in detailing how damaging long term, severe bullying can be to a person. Brain scans show scientifically how bullying can and does negatively impact the brain. Post-traumatic stress disorder or PTSD is a real concern for those who subjected to relentless taunts, degrading put-downs or even physical assault.

As bad as all that is for those who are bullied, imagine someone who is bullied by his or her buddy. Not only does he or she experience all of the above, but also has to deal with the betrayal of someone he or she trusted to be a friend. The passive-aggressive nature of the flip flopping from nice to mean can be confusing. Sometimes the bullying is disguised, such as a mean remark or taunt followed by a "just kidding," leaving a person confused about where he or she stands in the friendship.

Certainly everyone has a mean moment now and again. Friends may say mean things to each other and then apologize and move on. Experiencing and resolving conflict is part of a healthy relationship and people are not always going to get along. It becomes bullying when the meanness is more deliberate and consistent and when the apologies stop. We encourage a child experiencing this to confront the friend who has done mean things. This way he or she can learn to defend his or herself against future issues (only if the child feels safe doing so). In order to approach a person who is acting like a bully, it's important to take enough time to calm down so as not to respond when emotions are raw.

Here is a scenario on how we might coach a child who is struggling with a meanie. We will say something to the effect of, "When you are defending yourself against a bully, you want to do your best not to cry or yell. You should try to very calmly, say 'Hey, I know that you guys all went to the movies without me. What's up with that?' The friend will likely feel taken aback and will probably come up with an excuse as to why you were not invited. What the response is from that person isn't as important as the fact that you called him or her out for his or her transgression. Saying nothing is implied permission that he or she can keep on doing things to you or excluding you because there are no consequences."

A child who doesn't have many friends may hang on to this type of friendship thinking that it's better than none at all. It's important for a child in this situation to understand that this "friend" is not, in fact, a friend. He or she is a bully in disguise. As much as he or she does not want to lose a "friend," he or she needs to separate from another child who is continuously belittling them and/or encouraging other children to do the same. If your child has a "frenemy" he or she will need your help to sort through the passive aggressive nature of the relationship.

It is never okay to be treated badly by anyone, especially someone who calls you, "friend."

It's Not Your Turn to be Happy

September 21, 2015 By Donna Shea

If we could all have our own way and have life exactly how we want it to be, wouldn't life be great? Of course, the problem quickly arises when we all want and enjoy different things.

This past summer at our camp program, I had one child in particular who had a very difficult time when we changed to any activity that he didn't enjoy. Sometimes it was the case of getting him to try it or watch it to see if we could coax him into something new. Many times, he just wanted our big recess room all to himself with activities of his choosing. When things didn't go the way he wanted them to, or it was announced that a new activity was to begin shortly, he would have a tantrum. There were times I fell into that tantrum trap and gave him what he wanted, only to realize that I was reinforcing a sense of entitlement and it became a pattern at camp that needed to change.

There came a day when there were lots of kids in the recess room. One little guy wanted me to play music and dance with him. When I turned on the music and we started to dance, my first friend yelled at us to stop. I turned to him and said, "Right now, it's not your turn to be happy. It's this guy's turn to be happy and do what he wants to do. I can understand that you might not like the noise or the music, so you are welcome to visit one of the other activity rooms until we are done." I find that that the power of social coaching a child lies in the ability to phrase things in a way that makes sense to the child and helps him or her adjust his or her thinking in the moment. Taking turns is something that most kids understand.

With that being said, I find that sharing is another area that we can assist a child in understanding and learning the important life skill that you can't always have what you want when you want it. For a long time, I felt that is was important to coach and teach kids how to share everything at my center. However, if we think about it, making a child who is playing with a toy or other object, share it simply because someone else wants it, creates entitlement. It gives the message to a child he or she can have whatever he or she wants just by saying so. So now, I tell the child who wants the toy that it is currently unavailable and that I can help him or her look for something else to play with. However, in many instances, taking turns is necessary and important to know how to do. If you have community toys or games, swings or other group items, set the rules for taking turns first. For example, each person has 5 minutes on the swings, or can ride the scooter around the playground 3 times before it someone else's turn.

The line between accommodating a child's needs and inadvertently creating a sense of entitlement is a fine one. To not always have what we want when we want it, or have the environment ideal to our own needs teaches us the important life skills of coping and frustration management. We can't always have what we want, and sometimes it's someone else's turn to be happy.

The True List

September 26, 2015 By Nadine Briggs

At my tween girls' social group this past week, I did an exercise where the girls were asked to make a True List.

A True List is a list of all their positive attributes. The middle school girls who attend my social group do not exhibit a very high levels of self-esteem, so I fully expected to see a few blank pieces of paper. I was pleasantly surprised to see that each girl had written down positive attributes about herself. Here is an example of one of the lists:

Friendly – Polite – Appreciative – Happy – Quiet – Outgoing – Sometimes Shy – Confident – Responsible – Goal-Oriented – Persistent – Beautiful – Brave – Strong – Powerful – Hard Worker – Loving – Sweet – Smart – Empathetic – Enthusiastic – Respectful – Proud – Helpful – Bright – Compassionate – Funny – Supportive – Talented – Independent

I talked about why would we do such an exercise and how we can use it in daily life. In middle school, the cliques and meanness are hard to avoid. Some might say that having times when a tween feels "less than" while in middle school is inevitable. I asked the group a few questions about their lists. If someone doesn't include you in a sleepover, which of these attributes should we delete? If someone doesn't want to hang out with you, does that mean this list doesn't apply to you anymore? Are you truly any less than or are you just being treated as if you are less than by the other girls? All the girls knew that the list of truths each had written about herself was indelible.

The list is a true list of each girl and who she is as a person. It is a list that no matter what happens or how she is treated or if she is or is not included, the list is still true and will always be true. I had each girl put the list in her backpack or enter it into her phone to keep that list with her at school. I then encouraged each girl to use that list in those moments when someone hurts her or treats her badly: to pull it out, read it again and know what is really true.

Watch Your Back at the Water Cooler: Friendships at Work

October 5, 2015 By Donna Shea

I know that our blog posts are usually about how to socially support children and teens. There have been circumstances recently at my center that prompt me to write a blog about adult friendships, especially those that form at work or through a working relationship. The combination of a personal friendship and a working relationship adds a degree of complexity that doesn't exist in friendships outside of work. The care and feeding of this type of friendship is very different, and having recently been through one, can be ripe for accidental or purposeful betrayals.

> A true friend is someone who says nice things behind your back.
>
> QuotesGate

I experienced the heart-crushing loss of a long-time friend and colleague over an issue that happened at work over the summer. The tears of anger and sadness came, and kept coming for most of the summer. Anger from the realization of the impact on the summer work schedule, and a deep painful sadness over the clear message that we were no longer friends and our families were no longer connected in the way they had been for many years. I searched my soul for what I did wrong or might have done differently. I thought maybe that with time, we might re-connect. With time, came acceptance and closure that it was what it was.

And then another wrenching blow came recently when I began to hear from other staff members things that were discussed or talked about behind my back, apparently for some time before all this happened. I believe I can solve any problem, if I know what it is. I have no patience or tolerance for water cooler gossip and I have told my staff this. I have begun to call out water cooler talk if I hear it at the office. It is human nature for us to talk about other people and I know that we are all guilty of it at one time or another. I have made it a mission to catch and stop myself when it happens and to bring awareness to my staff when it occurs at work. If a person isn't present, that person is not to be discussed.

Problems at work arise. People are not compatible or disagree on how things should be handled. Some work harder than others. A person may not know that there is something that needs to be worked on or changed. Talking about it behind that person's back will never see any changes or improvements discussed or implemented. Staff meetings should and will become part of our business at the center now as we have grown enough to reach the point where there are enough people and personalities that invite this type of talking about each other. I won't have it in a place who's business it is to promote kindness, good manners and conflict resolution.

Nadine and I are often asked how we manage to maintain such a close friendship and be managing partners of a company while also running centers that could be considered competitive with each other if we allowed that type of thinking. It takes the same type of working at it as does a marriage. We don't always agree. We compromise or take turns having our way. We have hurt each other's feelings. We apologize or take time to explore a misunderstanding. We don't compete. We believe there is an abundance of kids that need help and support each other wholeheartedly. We give credit where credit is due for each other's work and projects.

Most importantly, (and I thank Nadine for teaching me this phrase), we know how to say, "We need to have an uncomfortable conversation," or one of us might also say to the other, "We should talk about this to prevent (as we like to call it) potential icky-ness," or sometimes we simply say, "Eeeeeek!" in a certain tone and the other knows to stop and listen. All of our problems are laid out, discussed and solved at our conference table and not hidden behind or covered up with mean talk at the water cooler. Nadine and I don't talk behind each other's back, we *have* each other's back.

Who Left the Chicken in the Chick Inn?

October 12, 2015 By Nadine Briggs

At my teen social groups this week, I wanted to teach the teens how to listen to and respond to a story that someone else thought was interesting – even if he or she didn't think it was interesting at all. In order to be approachable and to be a person who other people want to engage in conversation, we need to understand that how we respond matters. The way we respond can determine if the person who has engaged us in conversation will decide whether or not he or she wants to continue to start up conversations with us in the future.

In order to be a good friend and be cognizant of other people's feelings, we occasionally need to act as though we are interested, even if it is a topic or story that doesn't interest us. To be a true friend, we need to know how to be engaging, ask questions, and make comments that add to what the person is telling us. I also help teens to understand that we should listen to, and match, the tone of the person talking to us. If he or she is excited, the response we give should be somewhat excited as well. If he or she is telling us something he or she thinks is shocking, we should respond as though we are also somewhat shocked. For kids and teens who are not naturally good at this aspect of conversation, it can take some practice to get the appropriate tone. I asked the teens to share interesting stories with the group so we could respond. If one of my groups couldn't think of any stories to share, it was their lucky day that day and they got to hear my own story of the mystery of how the chicken got into the Chick Inn.

My story requires some background explanation which gave the teens more experience in learning to listen to the background of a story so it will make sense to them. My teens usually get bored easily, but I was pleased to see how well they did with this exercise. Here's the story:

The group of friends who I
hang out with regularly are
referred to as the Chickies.
We have game nights and
movie nights and generally
have a great time together.
Because I live near wetlands and the mosquitoes are
really bad in the summertime, I have a cabana with
screened in walls in my yard. It's sort of my "lady
cave." It's a peaceful place to hang out and it's
awesome when the solar lights come on at dusk. And
it's called the Chick Inn (of course!)

During the recent eclipse,
my husband and I went
outside to watch it in the
Chick Inn. As I got closer
to the cabana, I realized
there was something
sitting on the coffee table. Much to my happy surprise
somebody had left a ceramic chicken in the Chick Inn.
I thought it was hysterically funny. The thought of one
of my friends creeping into my yard in the dead of
night and leaving this unexpected gift on my table
amused me to no end. The puns on social media were
endless:

"The plot chickens."

"Nadine is ruffling some feathers."

"Clearly someone is egging you on."

"Eggs-specting some chickie will crack the case."

"I'm pecking around to see what I can find out."

The teens responded so well to listening and interacting with my story that I couldn't tell if they were truly interested or if they had just mastered this activity. They asked questions about who lives close by, were any clues left behind, had I dusted for fingerprints, who knew when I was home and so on. All the groups did a great job of making conversation about the whodunit.

But the question still remains, who left the chicken in the Chick Inn?

Perspective That Hits Like a Mack Truck

November 2, 2015 By Nadine Briggs

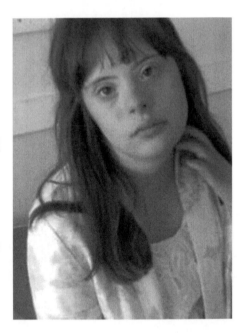

As some of you know, my 18-year-old daughter, Megan, has Down syndrome and attends a residential school about 90 minutes from our home. Being Megan's mother has given me much joy but has also given me a vast amount of experience in solving challenging problems. Lots and lots of very complicated, intertwined problems for which there are usually multiple causes and complex solutions. Megan was home this week as we were in the throes of such a problem. A medically complex but not dangerous problem.

Then the news hit that one of her closest friends passed away in her sleep at school. We had just seen her laughing and dancing the week before, seemingly happy and healthy, and just like that, she was gone forever.

My daughter understands death. She knows exactly what it means. Her level of compassion for others is unmatched. She is deeply saddened by her own loss but thinks of the family's grief alongside her own.

Perspective came like a Mack truck. A lightning bolt to my soul. We'll figure out whatever we have to figure out. We always have and we always will. The problem solving or acceptance of the problem may happen at 4:00 am but it will happen.

My daughter has what she calls "moments" when she needs to grieve. She cries and she needs the arms of those who love and understand her to hold her close. During those times, as I hold her even closer, what she doesn't realize, is that I'm having a moment of my own.

The Sinking (Friend)Ship of Self Amusement

November 9, 2015 By Donna Shea

Marcus is running into a group of kids playing a game with a ball, takes the ball and gleefully runs away with it. When asked if he wants to join the game, he says no and continues to disrupt the game.

Angie is hurling what she thinks are funny, but are actually annoying comments at another teen, and doesn't stop when the other teen becomes agitated and angry.

Joey is playing Wii with three other boys and repeatedly presses the pause button during the game or changes the game options despite continuous pleas to knock it off.

One of the important aspects of social coaching and helping kids make and keep friends, is observing when and how kids may be contributing to their own social difficulties. A child or teen indulging in actions for his or her own self amusement is an area of coaching that pops up frequently. Usually, these kids are seeking the stimulation of a reaction from other people. Calling this out can go something like this: "I have been listening (or watching) and see that it may feel fun to _____. The problem is that the other person is (or players are) growing annoyed and angry. I want to point out that there is a big risk of losing a friend (or a potential) friend if it continues and the consequences of choosing to keep doing _____ should be considered if it doesn't stop.

This is a different situation than the child or teen who is not aware that his or her actions are causing social difficulty and we coach those situations in other ways, with strategies on how to join a group, adjusting tone of voice and playing a game fairly. In the coaching instances mentioned previously, it is a child or teen that is actively seeking the stimulation of self-amusement despite coaching or social feedback from the other kids. It is important for these kids to understand how those choices can sabotage and sink a friendship or potential friendship.

When the Heart Hides

November 15, 2015 By Nadine Briggs

She can be really tough, even downright mean at times. She is openly abrasive and does not care what others think of her. She's going to do what she wants and no one can stop her. She has a *"take that, world!"* attitude.

The door to her heart is iron clad steel. She has totally closed off so that no one can get in. She will make sure that no one will even want to. She figures that by striking out first, she stays in control. Supposed *friends* who became bullies did this to her. Openly blatant, bold faced, "let's Instagram it" middle school rejection created that steel door. She believes no one can hurt her if she is the one doing the hurting.

There is a flaw in her plan. I know something about her that she does not show and I am telling. Are you ready? She is really nice! She is sweet and she cares deeply about others. She has a huge heart and she works very hard to protect it. Sometimes I think she works so hard at being tough that she forgets who she really is on the inside. So I keep telling her. I've been telling her for years. I tell her I know she has been hurt and I know she never wants to feel that way again. I also tell her that she matters.

Part of being strong is showing who you really are and not backing down. Kindness is not weakness. Kindness is more empowering than toughness. She is beginning to understand. The steel door is opening and she is peeking around to the other side. She is showing her heart and she is seeing that others truly like and enjoy this side of her. True friends, real friends are helping her to feel safe again. She is finding the courage to put her soul on display for all to see and it is simply beautiful to see.

Look for the heart of a tough, angry child or teen. You will likely find the gifts hidden inside.

How do *you* eat an ice cream sandwich?

November 23, 2015 By Donna Shea

We work with many kids who might be described as inflexible or rigid in their thinking.

There are times when a one-track mind is a powerfully positive force, staying with a task until completed, or an amazing idea until it comes to fruition. There are other times when a brain that has a difficult time bending to see other perspectives or solutions can be a source of frustration for the child or those with whom that child interacts. A child may have a difficult time understanding or even considering that there are different ways of going about things, none of them right or wrong, or better or worse then any other, just different.

The gal on my mind as I write this is a tween who I had in a social group awhile back. She was a terrific young lady, who approached the world in her own unique and amazing way and had interests that veered away from the usual tween fare. Incredibly intelligent and thoughtful, she often challenged me to consider my approach to supporting kids on the spectrum and to really, really listen to and to appreciate and celebrate the differences in the way we think about things.

I remember a day when I was serving ice cream sandwiches as an early summer treat and the kids were happily removing the wrappers completely (or not), breaking them in half (or not), licking around the sides first or simply just munching away. This young lady had been out of the room and when she returned, became quite distraught. She exclaimed, "that is NOT how you eat an ice cream sandwich!" Her distress was clear. I had a great group of kids, so no one reacted in any way except with puzzlement.

I asked her, "how do *you* eat an ice cream sandwich?" When her response was on a paper plate, with a fork, peeling away the top layer, then the ice cream and then the bottom layer, I happily accommodated her ice cream sandwich style with the plate and fork. While we were all enjoying our treat in our various ways, I used it as a social lesson on several fronts: accommodating the needs of others, making room for different ways that we each approach something, and that there is not a right way or a wrong way, but many ways to eat an ice cream sandwich.

Top 5 Social Skills Games for Your Holiday Shopping List

November 29, 2015 By Nadine Briggs

In our work as social coaches, we offer a variety of toys and games for the kids to play with to keep things interesting and create a fun environment. All toys and games have a social element to them where we encourage sharing and good sportsmanship but we have a few favorites that we use with a purpose. Here is our list and why you may want to add them to your holiday shopping list this season.

1) Whoonu by Cranium Product Description: The what's your favorite thing game. You're sure to have unforgettable fun as you reveal your favorite things, share hilarious stories, and bond over surprising

connections. You'll be amazed at what you'll learn about your friends and family — especially those you think you know best! Whoonu is easy to learn and quick to play, so it's the perfect game for any occasion. And best of all, it's just as fun to play with people you've known for 5 minutes as it is with people you've known forever! Game includes 300 game cards, 36 scoring tokens and a secret envelope. Game takes approximately 15 minutes to play. For 3 to 6 players.

Why We Like It: This game is designed so that players rank the favorite things of other players. It is a great way to get kids to think about what others are thinking (perspective taking). If kids know each other well, they will likely do well in the game and if they aren't familiar with one another, they will have a better understanding of likes and dislikes after playing this game.

2) Bubble Talk
Product

Description: Bubble Talk is a new fast-paced family board game that asks players to match hilarious captions with funny pictures. A game that is as much fun if you are 8 or 80. The game begins when each player draws seven random caption cards. The judge for that round draws a picture card and players must quickly try to match

the funniest caption they have to the picture. The player who makes the judge laugh the most wins that round. Each round provides comical, clever and creative results, guaranteed to keep everyone laughing. Perfect for a small group of three or as many as eight players. Each game includes 150 picture cards (4"x 6") and 300 hilarious caption cards that allow for hours of game play. So let's get started!

Why We Like It: The kids absolutely love this game. It always generates peals of laughter. The game has photos of rather odd scenarios with a wide variety of captions that may go with the images. Kids will practice respecting the opinion of peers as the "it" for the round chooses the caption that they think fits the image best. Some of the captions may be a bit "edgy" for younger kids so we remove those from the game.

3) Apples to Apples

Product Description: The name of the game is a play on the phrase "apples to oranges," and the game is about making comparisons between different things. General game play is as

follows: players are dealt red cards which have a noun printed on them, and the judge (a different player in each turn) draws a green card on which an adjective is printed and places it for all players to see. Each player then chooses a red card they are holding that they think best describes the green card. The judge then decides which adjective she likes best.

Why We Like It: This game is a classic that is just like Bubble Talk only with words.

4) Boochie Ball

Product Description: Get ready for this all new action-packed family game that will have you tossing, kicking, bowling, and throwing like never before! First toss out

the soft foam Boochie target and then try to land your ball and hoop as close to it as possible. Keep score on a special wrist tracker that gives you a different outrageous throwing challenge every round. You may have to toss between your legs, behind your back, or even with your eyes closed! The player with the most points wins. Play Boochie... Have a ball! 2-4 players. Playing time about 15 minutes. Contents: 4 toss rings,

4 bean balls, 4 wrist trackers, 1 12-sided Boochie Ball, Vinyl Travel bag. AWARDS: Oppenheim Toy Portfolio Gold Award, iParenting Media Award, National Parenting Center Seal of Approval, Major Fun Award, Parents' Choice Silver Honor, Dr. Toy's Best Product Award Winner, Creative Child Magazine Game of the Year, National Parenting Publications (NAPPA) Gold Award.

Why We Like It: Boochie Ball requires a bit of space but can be played inside. Kids wear a wrist band that explains how they will take their next turn. It helps teach the concept that fair isn't always equal.

5) Likewise

Product Description: Likewise is a lively party game where it pays to think alike! One player turns over a "description" card and a "subject" card to create a zany category like "Goofy" "Hairstyle." Then each player writes something that fits that category on their paddle without showing anyone else. When everyone is done writing, players flip over their paddles to reveal their answers. The most matched answer wins the round! Think you know which "Outrageous" "Celebrity" your best friend would choose? How about which "Mysterious" "Cooking Utensil" or "Pathetic" "Politician"? There are over 5,000 possible category combinations! The more you think like the other players, the more likely you are to win the game! Recommended for 3 to 6 players, ages 14+. Contents include 6 paddles, 6 dry erase markers, 71 description cards, 71 subject cards, scoreboard, die and stickers.

Why we Like It: Kids connect with other kids who have the same answers forming a stronger friendship bond.

Games that do not have "screens" are generally the best for encouraging strong socialization. Happy holidays! Note: Descriptions are from Amazon.com

Naughty or Nice?

December 6, 2015 By Donna Shea

The season has arrived when helping kids with behavior management includes elves on shelves and being on the naughty or nice list. Children are cautioned to be good girls and boys.

As the adults, we need to be cautious too. Cautious about labeling a child as good or bad, nice or naughty. I know children that have labeled themselves in negative terms based on the messages given to them over time and damage to self-esteem can be quite extensive. We can and should however, label the *behaviors* that a child is engaged in and choices that he or she is making and assist a child in learning a better, and more effective way, of communicating.

Some examples:

"You are being rude and disrespectful!" could be changed to, "That tone of voice sounds rude and is hard for me to listen to. Let's try again."

"Quit whining!" could become, "My ears can't listen as well to a whining voice. What does a big kid voice sound like?"

"You're a bad boy (or girl!)" in a different way would be, "This is not a good choice that is being made right now, what would be a better one?"

Another phrase that we as adults may use frequently is "be a good girl (or boy)." If we think about it, that is a very broad statement that we expect kids to interpret the meaning of. A more effective way to elicit the behaviors that you want from a child is to clearly state your expectations for a given situation.

Some examples:

"When we are in the grocery store, I expect you to stay by the cart, not take anything off the shelves, and to choose only one special treat."

"We are going into the library and I expect that we will remember the rules about being quiet, listening to the librarian and putting our books back on the shelves when we are done."

"At Grandma's house tonight, I expect that you will be use polite words and table manners during dinner." (You may also want to give a child a refresher on the specifics of table manners.) The more we can break it down, the more the child will understand our expectations.

Elves on shelves are fun, and Santa's naughty or nice list can buy us good behavior for a few weeks. In changing our language, we can help children manage their behavior choices all year long.

5 Tips for Sensory Sensitive Children During the Holidays

December 14, 2015 By Nadine Briggs

The holidays can be challenging for kids who experience sensory sensitivities. The pressure is on for  families to enjoy being together, but the environment can be ripe for a sensory meltdown. Christmas lights, different types of food, overheated and crowded rooms with groups of people gathering together, the excitement of gift giving, uncomfortable dress clothes and more. Toss in a relative that the child rarely sees who wants a hug or kiss and you just might be dealing with a full blown sensory meltdown. Here are 5 tips to prepare for and hopefully prevent sensory overload this holiday season.

1. **Explain to your child what to expect** – children who are caught off guard by sensory input are more likely to meltdown than those

who have had time to mentally prepare. By explaining to your child what to expect, you and your child can map out strategies for what to do when he or she needs a break from all of the noise or excitement.

2. **Contact the host family ahead of time** – contact the family member who is hosting the gathering ahead of time and explain that your child may need a designated quiet place to retreat to for short periods of time. Once you work out where that area or room is located, show your child the area before it is needed so he or she can acclimate to the environment.

3. **Bring food that he or she likes** – it would be great if your child could eat the food prepared by the host and certainly ask your child to give it a try, but bring foods along with you that you know he or she will eat. It is better to feed your child a known food that he or she enjoys, rather than to experience a meltdown due to hunger or because he or she feels forced to eat food that makes him or her uncomfortable.

4. **Dress your child in layers** – rooms with a lot of people can heat up quickly, so dressing in layers allows your child the option of shedding

the extra clothing to maintain a comfortable body temperature.

5. **Be polite but firm** – Family members may not understand what your child needs to enjoy the event and they may, unwittingly, cause your best laid plans to go awry. Be friendly and polite with family members, but remain firm with what your child needs. For example, if your child is afraid of dogs, holiday gatherings are not the time to attempt dog immersion therapy.

If all else fails, you may need to be prepared to bring your sensory-sensitive child home while the rest of the family stays. What is fun for most kids just may not be fun at all for your sensitive child. If things are not working, there is no shame is heading home on the early side. We each have our own sensory tolerance levels and everyone should be respectful of sensory limits.

The Art of Giving and Receiving

December 21, 2015 By Donna Shea

'Tis the season of gift giving. In my social skills groups this past week, we have been talking about and practicing the tips in our book in the section on giving and receiving gifts and we are happy to share an excerpt from our book for kids with you!

Social Situation #36

Giving and Receiving Gifts

Friends and family often give each other gifts. You might be invited to a holiday party or having one of your own. It is important to know the social rules about giving and receiving gifts so that when you choose a gift for someone else, that person knows that you put thought into it. It is also important that you protect another person's feelings if that person gives you a gift that you already have or do not like.

- When you choose a gift for someone, think about what he or she is interested in or what he or she enjoys.
- When you give a gift to someone, say something such as "I got this for you and I hope you like it."
- When someone thanks you for a gift, remember to say "You're welcome."
- When someone is giving you a gift, wait for him or her to hand it to you and take it gently.
- Remember to say "Thank you" and smile when someone hands you a gift.
- Open the gift carefully.
- Grabbing gifts and tearing into paper is considered rude. Helping someone else open a gift is also considered rude unless he or she has asked for your help.
- If the gift is something that you already have, just say "Thank you." If the person asks you if you already have one and would like to exchange it, then it is fine to say that you do.
- If the gift is something you do not like, this is a situation where it is important that you pretend to like it and say "Thank you." It is never okay to tell a person that you do not like the gift that he or she gave you. Pretending is allowed when you receive gifts to protect the other person's feelings.

- Send a thank you note for the gift to let the person who gave you the gift know how much you enjoyed it.

About the Authors

Donna Shea and Nadine Briggs are both accomplished social educators. They each facilitate friendship groups at their respective centers in Massachusetts. Both Donna and Nadine are parents of children with special needs.

Donna and Nadine consult with schools, parent groups, and human service agencies. They are also seasoned public speakers and travel to bring workshops and to schools, conferences and other venues across the country. Both Donna and Nadine are certified in bullying prevention through the Massachusetts Aggression Reduction Center and are creators of the How to Make & Keep Friends Social Success in School Bullying Prevention Initiative to provide classroom training for school systems.

We would love to hear your feedback on our books, speak with you about providing programming in your area or keep in touch with you about new books and materials.

Find us on Facebook or:
Email us: howtomakeandkeepfriends@gmail.com

Printed in Great Britain
by Amazon